EMPLOYER COSTS FOR EMPLOYEE COMPENSATION – DECEMBER 2014

Private industry employers spent an average of $31.32 per hour worked for total employee compensation in December 2014, the U.S. Bureau of Labor Statistics reported today. Wages and salaries averaged $21.72 per hour worked and accounted for 69.4 percent of these costs, while benefits averaged $9.60 and accounted for the remaining 30.6 percent. Total compensation costs for **state and local government** workers averaged $43.95 per hour worked in December 2014. Total employer compensation costs for **civilian** workers, which include private industry and state and local government workers, averaged $33.13 per hour worked in December 2014.

Employer Costs for Employee Compensation (ECEC), a product of the National Compensation Survey, measures employer costs for wages, salaries, and employee benefits for nonfarm private and state and local government workers.

Chart 1. Employer costs per hour worked for paid leave by full-time and part-time status and all workers, private industry, December 2014

Cost per hour worked

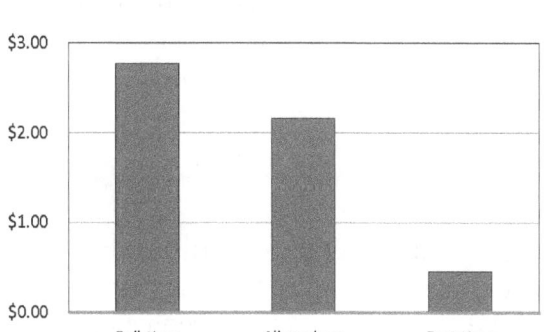

Chart 2. Employer costs per hour worked for legally required benefits by selected major industry group and all workers, private industry, December 2014

Cost per hour worked

Paid leave costs in private industry

Private industry employer costs for paid leave benefits averaged $2.16 per hour worked in December 2014. Private industry costs for paid leave include **vacation** leave which averaged $1.13 per hour worked, **holiday** leave which averaged 66 cents, **sick** leave which averaged 26 cents, and **personal** leave which averaged 12 cents in December 2014. Paid leave benefit costs are often directly linked to wages; therefore, higher paid occupations or industries will typically show higher estimates for this compensation component.

Private industry **paid leave** benefit costs were highest for management, professional, and related occupations at $4.67 per hour worked, or 8.4 percent of total compensation, in December 2014. Costs were lowest among service occupations at 56 cents, or 3.9 percent of total compensation. (See table 5.) Included in this amount were employer costs for vacations, holidays, sick leave, and personal leave.

The average cost per hour worked for **paid leave** by major industry group ranged from $4.82 in information to 41 cents in leisure and hospitality. (See table 6.)

Paid leave costs varied widely by full-time and part-time status in private industry in December 2014. Paid leave costs for full-time workers were $2.77 per hour worked versus 45 cents for part-time workers. (See chart 1 and table 12.)

For information on **paid leave** provisions, see *National Compensation Survey: Employee Benefits in the United States, March 2014,* at www.bls.gov/ncs/ebs/benefits/2014/benefits.htm.

Legally required benefit costs in private industry

The average cost for **legally required benefits** was $2.50 per hour worked in private industry (8.0 percent of total compensation) in December 2014. Social Security comprises the largest legally required benefit cost component at $1.44 per hour or 4.6 percent of total compensation. Legally required benefits such as Social Security and Medicare are often directly linked to wages; therefore, higher paid occupations or industries will typically show higher cost estimates for this compensation component. (See table 5.)

Costs for other **legally required benefits** include **workers' compensation** which averaged 44 cents per hour worked (1.4 percent of total compensation), **state unemployment insurance** which averaged 22 cents per hour worked (0.7 percent), and **federal unemployment insurance** which averaged just 4 cents per hour worked (0.1 percent). (See table 5.)

The average cost per hour worked for **legally required benefits** by major industry group ranged from $3.80 for construction industry workers to $1.40 per hour for leisure and hospitality. For construction industry workers, workers' compensation costs averaged $1.32 per hour worked, significantly higher than all other major industry groups. The proportion of total compensation represented by legally required benefits ranged from 10.6 percent for leisure and hospitality workers to 6.4 percent for both information and financial activities workers. (See chart 2 and table 6.)

Other benefit categories in private industry

Private industry employer costs averaged $2.54 per hour worked for **insurance** benefits (life, health, and disability insurance), or 8.1 percent of total compensation. In addition to insurance, the other benefit categories were: **supplemental pay** (overtime and premium, shift differentials, and nonproduction bonuses), which averaged $1.10 per hour worked (3.5 percent); and **retirement and savings**, which averaged $1.30 per hour (4.2 percent). (See table A and table 5.)

Table A. Relative importance of employer costs for employee compensation, December 2014

Compensation component	Civilian workers	Private industry	State and local government
Wages and salaries	68.4%	69.4%	64.1%
Benefits	31.6	30.6	35.9
Paid leave	7.0	6.9	7.3
Supplemental pay	3.0	3.5	0.8
Insurance	8.8	8.1	11.9
Health benefits	8.4	7.6	11.6
Retirement and savings	5.3	4.2	10.1
Defined benefit	3.3	2.0	9.2
Defined contribution	1.9	2.2	0.9
Legally required	7.6	8.0	5.9

The Employer Costs for Employee Compensation for March 2015 is scheduled to be released on Wednesday, June 10, 2015, at 10:00 a.m. (EDT).

Employer Costs for Employee Compensation data on total compensation, wages and salaries, and benefits in private industry are produced annually for 15 metropolitan areas. Metropolitan area data will be included in the March 2015 news release on June 10, 2015. For further information about metropolitan area ECEC estimates see the September 2009 article: "BLS Introduces New Employer Costs for Employee Compensation Data for Private Industry Workers in 15 Metropolitan Areas," at www.bls.gov/opub/mlr/cwc/bls-introduces-new-employer-costs-for-employee-compensation-data-for-private-industry-workers-in-15-metropolitan-areas.pdf.

Supplemental tables with occupational, establishment size, and bargaining status series for detailed industries are available at www.bls.gov/ncs/ect/sp/ecsuphst.pdf and www.bls.gov/ncs/ect/sp/ecsuptc33.pdf.

Relative standard errors for all cost estimates in the most recent news release and supplementary tables are available at www.bls.gov/ncs/ect/sp/ecsuprse.pdf.

Historical ECEC data are available in three listings, all available at www.bls.gov/ect/#tables. The first historical listing covers data for the March reference periods from 1986 to 2001. These data use the Standard Industrial Classification (SIC) and Census of Population occupational classification systems. The second listing contains data for the March, June, September, and December reference periods from March 2002 to December 2003. These data are also based on the SIC and Census of Population occupational classification systems. The final listing includes data for March 2004 to the current reference period. These are based on the North American Industry Classification System (NAICS) and Standard Occupational Classification (SOC) systems.

Information in this release will be made available to sensory impaired individuals upon request— Telephone: (202) 691-5200; Federal Relay Service: (800) 877-8339.

BLS news releases, including the ECEC, are available through an e-mail subscription service at: www.bls.gov/bls/list.htm.

TECHNICAL NOTE

Employer Costs for Employee Compensation (ECEC) measures the average cost to employers for wages and salaries and benefits per employee hour worked.

ECEC includes the civilian economy, which includes data from both private industry and state and local government. Excluded from private industry are the self-employed and farm and private household workers. Federal government workers are excluded from the public sector. The private industry series and the state and local government series provide data for the two sectors separately.

Sample size

Data for the December 2014 reference period were collected from a probability sample of approximately 37,700 occupational observations selected from a sample of about 8,700 private industry establishments and approximately 9,000 occupational observations selected from a sample of about 1,500 state and local government establishments that provided data at the initial interview.

Comparing private and public sector data

Compensation cost levels in state and local government should not be directly compared with levels in private industry. Differences between these sectors stem from factors such as variation in work activities and occupational structures. Manufacturing and sales, for example, make up a large part of private industry work activities but are rare in state and local government. Professional and administrative support occupations (including teachers) account for two-thirds of the state and local government workforce, compared with one-half of private industry.

ECEC quarterly publication focus

ECEC news releases are published quarterly, providing estimates on civilian, private industry, and state and local government cost per hour worked as well as additional detail on a specific compensation cost topic of interest. This quarter focuses on paid leave and legally required benefits costs in private industry. Topics of news releases for the upcoming reference periods are as follows:
- March 2015—Health benefit costs in private industry
- June 2015—Retirement and savings benefit costs in private industry
- September 2015—Compensation costs in state and local government

ECEC detailed information and measures

For detailed information on the Employer Costs for Employee Compensation, see Chapter 8, "National Compensation Measures," in the *BLS Handbook of Methods* at: www.bls.gov/opub/hom/pdf/homch8.pdf.

Table 1. Employer costs per hour worked for employee compensation and costs as a percent of total compensation: Civilian workers, by major occupational and industry group, December 2014

Compensation component	All workers[1]		Management, professional, and related		Sales and office		Service	
	Cost	Percent	Cost	Percent	Cost	Percent	Cost	Percent
Total compensation	$33.13	100.0	$54.95	100.0	$24.10	100.0	$17.03	100.0
Wages and salaries	22.65	68.4	37.45	68.2	16.90	70.2	12.11	71.1
Total benefits	10.49	31.6	17.50	31.8	7.19	29.8	4.92	28.9
Paid leave	2.31	7.0	4.38	8.0	1.57	6.5	0.89	5.2
Vacation	1.13	3.4	2.13	3.9	0.78	3.2	0.42	2.5
Holiday	0.70	2.1	1.27	2.3	0.48	2.0	0.28	1.6
Sick	0.35	1.0	0.72	1.3	0.21	0.9	0.14	0.8
Personal	0.13	0.4	0.26	0.5	0.09	0.4	0.05	0.3
Supplemental pay	0.99	3.0	1.87	3.4	0.55	2.3	0.29	1.7
Overtime and premium[4]	0.25	0.8	0.15	0.3	0.15	0.6	0.15	0.9
Shift differentials	0.06	0.2	0.08	0.1	0.02	0.1	0.05	0.3
Nonproduction bonuses	0.68	2.1	1.64	3.0	0.38	1.6	0.09	0.5
Insurance	2.92	8.8	4.40	8.0	2.35	9.7	1.40	8.2
Life	0.05	0.1	0.08	0.1	0.03	0.1	0.02	0.1
Health	2.78	8.4	4.16	7.6	2.25	9.3	1.36	8.0
Short-term disability	0.05	0.2	0.08	0.2	0.04	0.2	0.02	0.1
Long-term disability	0.05	0.1	0.08	0.1	0.03	0.1	([5])	([6])
Retirement and savings	1.75	5.3	3.37	6.1	0.86	3.6	0.74	4.4
Defined benefit	1.11	3.3	2.11	3.8	0.43	1.8	0.60	3.5
Defined contribution	0.64	1.9	1.27	2.3	0.43	1.8	0.14	0.8
Legally required benefits	2.51	7.6	3.48	6.3	1.87	7.7	1.61	9.4
Social Security and Medicare	1.82	5.5	2.90	5.3	1.40	5.8	1.00	5.9
Social Security[7]	1.45	4.4	2.27	4.1	1.13	4.7	0.80	4.7
Medicare	0.37	1.1	0.63	1.1	0.27	1.1	0.20	1.2
Federal unemployment insurance	0.03	0.1	0.03	([6])	0.04	0.2	0.04	0.2
State unemployment insurance	0.20	0.6	0.18	0.3	0.19	0.8	0.18	1.0
Workers' compensation	0.45	1.4	0.37	0.7	0.23	1.0	0.39	2.3

See footnotes at end of table.

Table 1. Employer costs per hour worked for employee compensation and costs as a percent of total compensation: Civilian workers, by major occupational and industry group, December 2014 — Continued

Compensation component	Occupational group				Industry group			
	Natural resources, construction, and maintenance		Production, transportation, and material moving		Goods-producing[2]		Service-providing[3]	
	Cost	Percent	Cost	Percent	Cost	Percent	Cost	Percent
Total compensation	$34.46	100.0	$27.05	100.0	$37.23	100.0	$32.42	100.0
Wages and salaries	22.70	65.9	17.73	65.5	24.58	66.0	22.31	68.8
Total benefits	11.76	34.1	9.32	34.5	12.64	34.0	10.11	31.2
Paid leave	1.93	5.6	1.66	6.1	2.45	6.6	2.29	7.1
Vacation	0.97	2.8	0.85	3.1	1.28	3.4	1.11	3.4
Holiday	0.63	1.8	0.55	2.0	0.85	2.3	0.67	2.1
Sick	0.21	0.6	0.20	0.7	0.23	0.6	0.37	1.1
Personal	0.12	0.3	0.07	0.2	0.09	0.2	0.14	0.4
Supplemental pay	0.99	2.9	0.99	3.7	1.48	4.0	0.91	2.8
Overtime and premium[4]	0.68	2.0	0.55	2.0	0.57	1.5	0.20	0.6
Shift differentials	0.05	0.1	0.08	0.3	0.08	0.2	0.05	0.2
Nonproduction bonuses	0.26	0.7	0.35	1.3	0.83	2.2	0.66	2.0
Insurance	3.26	9.4	2.95	10.9	3.48	9.4	2.82	8.7
Life	0.04	0.1	0.04	0.2	0.07	0.2	0.04	0.1
Health	3.09	9.0	2.78	10.3	3.28	8.8	2.69	8.3
Short-term disability	0.09	0.3	0.06	0.2	0.08	0.2	0.05	0.2
Long-term disability	0.04	0.1	0.07	0.3	0.06	0.1	0.05	0.1
Retirement and savings	2.32	6.7	1.16	4.3	2.05	5.5	1.70	5.2
Defined benefit	1.72	5.0	0.67	2.5	1.18	3.2	1.10	3.4
Defined contribution	0.60	1.7	0.49	1.8	0.87	2.3	0.60	1.9
Legally required benefits	3.26	9.5	2.57	9.5	3.18	8.5	2.39	7.4
Social Security and Medicare	1.92	5.6	1.51	5.6	2.09	5.6	1.78	5.5
Social Security[7]	1.55	4.5	1.22	4.5	1.68	4.5	1.41	4.3
Medicare	0.37	1.1	0.29	1.1	0.41	1.1	0.37	1.1
Federal unemployment insurance	0.03	0.1	0.04	0.1	0.03	0.1	0.03	0.1
State unemployment insurance	0.28	0.8	0.23	0.9	0.28	0.7	0.19	0.6
Workers' compensation	1.03	3.0	0.79	2.9	0.78	2.1	0.40	1.2

[1] Includes workers in the private nonfarm economy excluding households and the public sector excluding the Federal government.
[2] Includes mining, construction, and manufacturing. The agriculture, forestry, farming, and hunting sector is excluded.
[3] Includes utilities; wholesale trade; retail trade; transportation and warehousing; information; finance and insurance; real estate and rental and leasing; professional and technical services; management of companies and enterprises; administrative and waste services; educational services; health care and social assistance; arts, entertainment and recreation; accommodation and food services; other services, except public administration; and public administration.
[4] Includes premium pay for work in addition to the regular work schedule (such as overtime, weekends, and holidays).
[5] Cost per hour worked is $0.01 or less.
[6] Less than .05 percent.
[7] Comprises the Old-Age, Survivors, and Disability Insurance (OASDI) program.

Note: The sum of individual items may not equal totals due to rounding.

Table 2. Employer costs per hour worked for employee compensation and costs as a percent of total compensation: Civilian workers, by occupational and industry group, December 2014

Series	Total compen-sation	Wages and salaries	Benefit costs					
			Total	Paid leave	Supple-mental pay	Insurance	Retire-ment and savings	Legally required benefits
			Cost per hour worked					
Civilian workers[1]	$33.13	$22.65	$10.49	$2.31	$0.99	$2.92	$1.75	$2.51
Occupational group								
Management, professional, and related	54.95	37.45	17.50	4.38	1.87	4.40	3.37	3.48
Management, business, and financial	65.50	43.60	21.89	5.83	3.91	4.54	3.57	4.04
Professional and related	50.40	34.80	15.60	3.75	1.00	4.34	3.29	3.24
Teachers[2]	56.36	39.74	16.62	2.75	0.17	5.43	5.15	3.12
Primary, secondary, and special education school teachers	56.71	39.09	17.62	2.49	0.17	6.36	5.78	2.82
Registered nurses	50.86	34.89	15.97	4.26	1.55	4.20	2.32	3.63
Sales and office	24.10	16.90	7.19	1.57	0.55	2.35	0.86	1.87
Sales and related	22.99	17.23	5.76	1.28	0.56	1.53	0.55	1.84
Office and administrative support	24.76	16.71	8.05	1.74	0.54	2.84	1.05	1.88
Service	17.03	12.11	4.92	0.89	0.29	1.40	0.74	1.61
Natural resources, construction, and maintenance	34.46	22.70	11.76	1.93	0.99	3.26	2.32	3.26
Construction, extraction, farming, fishing, and forestry[3]	35.00	22.87	12.12	1.52	0.91	3.29	2.71	3.69
Installation, maintenance, and repair	33.99	22.55	11.45	2.28	1.06	3.22	1.99	2.90
Production, transportation, and material moving	27.05	17.73	9.32	1.66	0.99	2.95	1.16	2.57
Production	26.53	17.53	8.99	1.68	1.15	2.84	0.92	2.40
Transportation and material moving	27.52	17.90	9.62	1.64	0.84	3.05	1.38	2.71
Industry group								
Education and health services	37.50	25.84	11.66	2.64	0.46	3.73	2.35	2.48
Educational services	45.58	31.06	14.52	2.78	0.18	4.97	3.99	2.60
Elementary and secondary schools	44.74	30.25	14.49	2.30	0.17	5.34	4.31	2.38
Junior colleges, colleges, and universities	49.99	34.18	15.80	4.01	0.18	4.66	3.88	3.08
Health care and social assistance	32.04	22.31	9.73	2.55	0.65	2.89	1.24	2.39
Hospitals	42.68	28.13	14.55	3.85	1.32	4.37	2.06	2.95
			Percent of total compensation					
Civilian workers[1]	100.0	68.4	31.6	7.0	3.0	8.8	5.3	7.6
Occupational group								
Management, professional, and related	100.0	68.2	31.8	8.0	3.4	8.0	6.1	6.3
Management, business, and financial	100.0	66.6	33.4	8.9	6.0	6.9	5.5	6.2
Professional and related	100.0	69.0	31.0	7.4	2.0	8.6	6.5	6.4
Teachers[2]	100.0	70.5	29.5	4.9	0.3	9.6	9.1	5.5
Primary, secondary, and special education school teachers	100.0	68.9	31.1	4.4	0.3	11.2	10.2	5.0
Registered nurses	100.0	68.6	31.4	8.4	3.1	8.3	4.6	7.1
Sales and office	100.0	70.2	29.8	6.5	2.3	9.7	3.6	7.7
Sales and related	100.0	74.9	25.1	5.6	2.5	6.6	2.4	8.0
Office and administrative support	100.0	67.5	32.5	7.0	2.2	11.5	4.2	7.6
Service	100.0	71.1	28.9	5.2	1.7	8.2	4.4	9.4
Natural resources, construction, and maintenance	100.0	65.9	34.1	5.6	2.9	9.4	6.7	9.5
Construction, extraction, farming, fishing, and forestry[3]	100.0	65.4	34.6	4.4	2.6	9.4	7.7	10.5
Installation, maintenance, and repair	100.0	66.3	33.7	6.7	3.1	9.5	5.9	8.5
Production, transportation, and material moving	100.0	65.5	34.5	6.1	3.7	10.9	4.3	9.5
Production	100.0	66.1	33.9	6.3	4.3	10.7	3.5	9.1
Transportation and material moving	100.0	65.0	35.0	6.0	3.1	11.1	5.0	9.9
Industry group								
Education and health services	100.0	68.9	31.1	7.0	1.2	10.0	6.3	6.6
Educational services	100.0	68.1	31.9	6.1	0.4	10.9	8.8	5.7
Elementary and secondary schools	100.0	67.6	32.4	5.1	0.4	11.9	9.6	5.3
Junior colleges, colleges, and universities	100.0	68.4	31.6	8.0	0.4	9.3	7.8	6.2
Health care and social assistance	100.0	69.6	30.4	8.0	2.0	9.0	3.9	7.5
Hospitals	100.0	65.9	34.1	9.0	3.1	10.2	4.8	6.9

[1] Includes workers in the private nonfarm economy excluding households and the public sector excluding the Federal government.
[2] Includes postsecondary teachers; primary, secondary, and special education teachers; and other teachers and instructors.
[3] Farming, fishing, and forestry occupations were combined with construction and extraction occupational group as of December 2006.

Note: The sum of individual items may not equal totals due to rounding.

Table 3. Employer costs per hour worked for employee compensation and costs as a percent of total compensation: State and local government workers, by major occupational and industry group, December 2014

Compensation component	All workers		Management, professional, and related		Sales and office		Service		Service-providing[2]	
	Cost	Percent	Cost	Percent	Cost	Percent	Cost	Percent	Cost	Percent
Total compensation	$43.95	100.0	$53.24	100.0	$30.18	100.0	$33.02	100.0	$44.00	100.0
Wages and salaries	28.17	64.1	35.52	66.7	18.01	59.7	19.24	58.3	28.23	64.2
Total benefits	15.78	35.9	17.72	33.3	12.16	40.3	13.78	41.7	15.77	35.8
Paid leave	3.20	7.3	3.54	6.7	2.62	8.7	2.87	8.7	3.20	7.3
Vacation	1.19	2.7	1.17	2.2	1.16	3.9	1.23	3.7	1.19	2.7
Holiday	0.95	2.2	1.00	1.9	0.82	2.7	0.91	2.8	0.94	2.1
Sick	0.84	1.9	1.06	2.0	0.51	1.7	0.58	1.8	0.84	1.9
Personal	0.23	0.5	0.31	0.6	0.12	0.4	0.14	0.4	0.23	0.5
Supplemental pay	0.35	0.8	0.26	0.5	0.20	0.7	0.60	1.8	0.35	0.8
Overtime and premium[3]	0.19	0.4	0.08	0.1	0.12	0.4	0.41	1.2	0.18	0.4
Shift differentials	0.04	0.1	0.03	0.1	0.02	0.1	0.09	0.3	0.04	0.1
Nonproduction bonuses	0.12	0.3	0.15	0.3	0.06	0.2	0.10	0.3	0.12	0.3
Insurance	5.22	11.9	5.70	10.7	4.73	15.7	4.39	13.3	5.22	11.9
Life	0.06	0.1	0.06	0.1	0.05	0.2	0.05	0.2	0.06	0.1
Health	5.09	11.6	5.55	10.4	4.63	15.3	4.29	13.0	5.09	11.6
Short-term disability	0.03	0.1	0.03	0.1	0.02	0.1	0.02	0.1	0.03	0.1
Long-term disability	0.04	0.1	0.05	0.1	0.03	0.1	0.02	0.1	0.04	0.1
Retirement and savings	4.42	10.1	5.26	9.9	2.72	9.0	3.80	11.5	4.42	10.0
Defined benefit	4.04	9.2	4.74	8.9	2.49	8.3	3.59	10.9	4.03	9.2
Defined contribution	0.38	0.9	0.52	1.0	0.23	0.8	0.21	0.6	0.38	0.9
Legally required benefits	2.59	5.9	2.96	5.6	1.89	6.3	2.13	6.5	2.59	5.9
Social Security and Medicare	1.95	4.4	2.37	4.4	1.42	4.7	1.38	4.2	1.95	4.4
Social Security[4]	1.50	3.4	1.80	3.4	1.12	3.7	1.06	3.2	1.50	3.4
Medicare	0.45	1.0	0.56	1.1	0.30	1.0	0.32	1.0	0.45	1.0
Federal unemployment insurance	([5])	([6])	([5])	([6])	([5])	([6])	([5])	([6])	([5])	([6])
State unemployment insurance	0.09	0.2	0.09	0.2	0.08	0.3	0.09	0.3	0.09	0.2
Workers' compensation	0.54	1.2	0.50	0.9	0.39	1.3	0.66	2.0	0.54	1.2

[1] This table presents data for the three major occupational groups in State and local government: management, professional, and related occupations, including teachers; sales and office occupations, including clerical workers; and service occupations, including police and firefighters.
[2] Service-providing industries, which include health and educational services, employ a large part of the State and local government workforce.
[3] Includes premium pay for work in addition to the regular work schedule (such as overtime, weekends, and holidays).
[4] Comprises the Old-Age, Survivors, and Disability Insurance (OASDI) program.
[5] Cost per hour worked is $0.01 or less.
[6] Less than .05 percent.

Note: The sum of individual items may not equal totals due to rounding.

Table 4. Employer costs per hour worked for employee compensation and costs as a percent of total compensation: State and local government workers, by occupational and industry group, December 2014

Series	Total compensation	Wages and salaries	Benefit costs					
			Total	Paid leave	Supplemental pay	Insurance	Retirement and savings	Legally required benefits
Cost per hour worked								
State and local government workers	$43.95	$28.17	$15.78	$3.20	$0.35	$5.22	$4.42	$2.59
Occupational group								
Management, professional, and related	53.24	35.52	17.72	3.54	0.26	5.70	5.26	2.96
Professional and related	52.32	35.16	17.16	3.20	0.25	5.66	5.21	2.84
Teachers[1]	60.04	41.66	18.37	2.90	0.15	6.11	6.11	3.10
Primary, secondary, and special education school teachers	60.01	41.12	18.88	2.59	0.17	6.78	6.45	2.89
Sales and office	30.18	18.01	12.16	2.62	0.20	4.73	2.72	1.89
Office and administrative support	30.35	18.08	12.27	2.65	0.20	4.79	2.74	1.90
Service	33.02	19.24	13.78	2.87	0.60	4.39	3.80	2.13
Industry group								
Education and health services	45.89	30.56	15.33	2.88	0.22	5.33	4.38	2.52
Educational services	46.64	31.26	15.38	2.73	0.16	5.41	4.58	2.50
Elementary and secondary schools	45.80	30.73	15.07	2.34	0.17	5.57	4.62	2.37
Junior colleges, colleges, and universities	49.55	33.19	16.36	3.97	0.13	4.83	4.53	2.91
Health care and social assistance	41.08	26.10	14.97	3.78	0.59	4.81	3.12	2.68
Hospitals	45.96	29.56	16.40	4.31	0.76	5.10	3.41	2.82
Public administration	42.04	24.94	17.10	3.90	0.59	5.17	4.71	2.73
Percent of total compensation								
State and local government workers	100.0	64.1	35.9	7.3	0.8	11.9	10.1	5.9
Occupational group								
Management, professional, and related	100.0	66.7	33.3	6.7	0.5	10.7	9.9	5.6
Professional and related	100.0	67.2	32.8	6.1	0.5	10.8	10.0	5.4
Teachers[1]	100.0	69.4	30.6	4.8	0.2	10.2	10.2	5.2
Primary, secondary, and special education school teachers	100.0	68.5	31.5	4.3	0.3	11.3	10.7	4.8
Sales and office	100.0	59.7	40.3	8.7	0.7	15.7	9.0	6.3
Office and administrative support	100.0	59.6	40.4	8.7	0.7	15.8	9.0	6.2
Service	100.0	58.3	41.7	8.7	1.8	13.3	11.5	6.5
Industry group								
Education and health services	100.0	66.6	33.4	6.3	0.5	11.6	9.5	5.5
Educational services	100.0	67.0	33.0	5.9	0.3	11.6	9.8	5.4
Elementary and secondary schools	100.0	67.1	32.9	5.1	0.4	12.2	10.1	5.2
Junior colleges, colleges, and universities	100.0	67.0	33.0	8.0	0.3	9.7	9.1	5.9
Health care and social assistance	100.0	63.5	36.5	9.2	1.4	11.7	7.6	6.5
Hospitals	100.0	64.3	35.7	9.4	1.7	11.1	7.4	6.1
Public administration	100.0	59.3	40.7	9.3	1.4	12.3	11.2	6.5

[1] Includes postsecondary teachers; primary, secondary, and special education teachers; and other teachers and instructors.

Note: The sum of individual items may not equal totals due to rounding.

Table 5. Employer costs per hour worked for employee compensation and costs as a percent of total compensation: Private industry workers, by major occupational group and bargaining unit status, December 2014

Compensation component	Occupational group							
	All workers		Management, professional, and related		Sales and office		Service	
	Cost	Percent	Cost	Percent	Cost	Percent	Cost	Percent
Total compensation	$31.32	100.0	$55.56	100.0	$23.57	100.0	$14.38	100.0
Wages and salaries	21.72	69.4	38.14	68.6	16.81	71.3	10.93	76.0
Total benefits	9.60	30.6	17.42	31.4	6.76	28.7	3.45	24.0
Paid leave	2.16	6.9	4.67	8.4	1.48	6.3	0.56	3.9
Vacation	1.13	3.6	2.46	4.4	0.75	3.2	0.29	2.0
Holiday	0.66	2.1	1.36	2.5	0.45	1.9	0.17	1.2
Sick	0.26	0.8	0.60	1.1	0.18	0.8	0.07	0.5
Personal	0.12	0.4	0.25	0.4	0.09	0.4	0.03	0.2
Supplemental pay	1.10	3.5	2.45	4.4	0.58	2.5	0.24	1.6
Overtime and premium[1]	0.26	0.8	0.18	0.3	0.15	0.6	0.11	0.7
Shift differentials	0.06	0.2	0.10	0.2	0.02	0.1	0.04	0.3
Nonproduction bonuses	0.78	2.5	2.17	3.9	0.41	1.7	0.08	0.6
Insurance	2.54	8.1	3.94	7.1	2.14	9.1	0.90	6.3
Life	0.04	0.1	0.09	0.2	0.03	0.1	([2])	([3])
Health	2.39	7.6	3.66	6.6	2.04	8.7	0.87	6.1
Short-term disability	0.06	0.2	0.10	0.2	0.04	0.2	([2])	([3])
Long-term disability	0.05	0.2	0.09	0.2	0.03	0.1	([2])	([3])
Retirement and savings	1.30	4.2	2.70	4.9	0.70	3.0	0.24	1.6
Defined benefit	0.62	2.0	1.17	2.1	0.25	1.1	0.10	0.7
Defined contribution	0.69	2.2	1.53	2.8	0.45	1.9	0.13	0.9
Legally required benefits	2.50	8.0	3.66	6.6	1.86	7.9	1.52	10.6
Social Security and Medicare	1.80	5.8	3.09	5.6	1.40	6.0	0.94	6.5
Social Security[4]	1.44	4.6	2.44	4.4	1.13	4.8	0.76	5.3
Medicare	0.36	1.2	0.65	1.2	0.27	1.2	0.18	1.2
Federal unemployment insurance	0.04	0.1	0.04	0.1	0.04	0.2	0.04	0.3
State unemployment insurance	0.22	0.7	0.22	0.4	0.20	0.9	0.19	1.3
Workers' compensation	0.44	1.4	0.32	0.6	0.22	0.9	0.35	2.4

See footnotes at end of table.

Table 5. Employer costs per hour worked for employee compensation and costs as a percent of total compensation: Private industry workers, by major occupational group and bargaining unit status, December 2014 — Continued

Compensation component	Occupational group				Bargaining unit status			
	Natural resources, construction, and maintenance		Production, transportation, and material moving		Union		Nonunion	
	Cost	Percent	Cost	Percent	Cost	Percent	Cost	Percent
Total compensation	$34.15	100.0	$26.83	100.0	$46.50	100.0	$29.83	100.0
Wages and salaries	22.76	66.7	17.67	65.9	27.76	59.7	21.13	70.8
Total benefits	11.39	33.3	9.16	34.1	18.74	40.3	8.70	29.2
Paid leave	1.79	5.2	1.63	6.1	3.25	7.0	2.05	6.9
Vacation	0.91	2.7	0.85	3.2	1.65	3.5	1.07	3.6
Holiday	0.59	1.7	0.54	2.0	0.95	2.0	0.63	2.1
Sick	0.17	0.5	0.18	0.7	0.48	1.0	0.24	0.8
Personal	0.12	0.3	0.06	0.2	0.17	0.4	0.11	0.4
Supplemental pay	1.03	3.0	1.01	3.8	1.44	3.1	1.07	3.6
Overtime and premium[1]	0.70	2.1	0.56	2.1	0.87	1.9	0.20	0.7
Shift differentials	0.05	0.1	0.09	0.3	0.18	0.4	0.05	0.2
Nonproduction bonuses	0.28	0.8	0.36	1.4	0.38	0.8	0.82	2.7
Insurance	3.08	9.0	2.86	10.7	6.01	12.9	2.20	7.4
Life	0.04	0.1	0.04	0.2	0.07	0.2	0.04	0.1
Health	2.91	8.5	2.69	10.0	5.64	12.1	2.07	6.9
Short-term disability	0.09	0.3	0.06	0.2	0.17	0.4	0.05	0.2
Long-term disability	0.03	0.1	0.08	0.3	0.13	0.3	0.04	0.1
Retirement and savings	2.16	6.3	1.09	4.0	4.38	9.4	1.00	3.4
Defined benefit	1.52	4.4	0.58	2.2	3.25	7.0	0.36	1.2
Defined contribution	0.64	1.9	0.51	1.9	1.13	2.4	0.64	2.2
Legally required benefits	3.33	9.8	2.57	9.6	3.66	7.9	2.38	8.0
Social Security and Medicare	1.94	5.7	1.51	5.6	2.30	4.9	1.75	5.9
Social Security[4]	1.57	4.6	1.22	4.5	1.83	3.9	1.40	4.7
Medicare	0.37	1.1	0.29	1.1	0.47	1.0	0.35	1.2
Federal unemployment insurance ...	0.03	0.1	0.04	0.1	0.04	0.1	0.04	0.1
State unemployment insurance ...	0.30	0.9	0.23	0.9	0.30	0.7	0.21	0.7
Workers' compensation	1.07	3.1	0.79	2.9	1.02	2.2	0.38	1.3

[1] Includes premium pay for work in addition to the regular work schedule (such as overtime, weekends, and holidays).
[2] Cost per hour worked is $0.01 or less.
[3] Less than .05 percent.
[4] Comprises the Old-Age, Survivors, and Disability Insurance (OASDI) program.

Note: The sum of individual items may not equal totals due to rounding.

Table 6. Employer costs per hour worked for employee compensation and costs as a percent of total compensation: Private industry workers, by major industry group, December 2014

Compensation component	Goods-producing[1]						Service-providing[2]					
	All goods-producing[1]		Construction		Manufacturing		All service-providing[2]		Trade, transportation, and utilities		Information	
	Cost	Percent	Cost	Percent	Cost	Percent	Cost	Percent	Cost	Percent	Cost	Percent
Total compensation	$37.21	100.0	$36.31	100.0	$36.73	100.0	$30.10	100.0	$25.74	100.0	$55.44	100.0
Wages and salaries	24.61	66.1	24.97	68.8	23.95	65.2	21.13	70.2	18.10	70.3	34.31	61.9
Total benefits	12.60	33.9	11.34	31.2	12.78	34.8	8.98	29.8	7.64	29.7	21.13	38.1
Paid leave	2.44	6.6	1.59	4.4	2.77	7.6	2.10	7.0	1.60	6.2	4.82	8.7
Vacation	1.27	3.4	0.82	2.2	1.45	3.9	1.09	3.6	0.86	3.3	2.50	4.5
Holiday	0.85	2.3	0.57	1.6	0.96	2.6	0.61	2.0	0.47	1.8	1.20	2.2
Sick	0.22	0.6	0.13	0.4	0.27	0.7	0.27	0.9	0.20	0.8	0.56	1.0
Personal	0.09	0.2	0.07	0.2	0.10	0.3	0.12	0.4	0.07	0.3	0.57	1.0
Supplemental pay	1.49	4.0	0.96	2.6	1.62	4.4	1.02	3.4	0.64	2.5	2.42	4.4
Overtime and premium[3]	0.57	1.5	0.60	1.6	0.53	1.4	0.20	0.7	0.27	1.0	0.35	0.6
Shift differentials	0.08	0.2	([4])	([5])	0.12	0.3	0.05	0.2	0.02	0.1	0.06	0.1
Nonproduction bonuses	0.84	2.3	0.35	1.0	0.97	2.6	0.77	2.5	0.35	1.3	2.00	3.6
Insurance	3.46	9.3	2.92	8.1	3.68	10.0	2.34	7.8	2.22	8.6	5.20	9.4
Life	0.07	0.2	0.04	0.1	0.07	0.2	0.04	0.1	0.03	0.1	0.06	0.1
Health	3.26	8.8	2.80	7.7	3.46	9.4	2.21	7.3	2.09	8.1	4.78	8.6
Short-term disability	0.08	0.2	0.05	0.1	0.09	0.2	0.05	0.2	0.04	0.1	0.27	0.5
Long-term disability	0.05	0.1	0.03	0.1	0.06	0.2	0.05	0.2	0.05	0.2	0.07	0.1
Retirement and savings	2.02	5.4	2.07	5.7	1.84	5.0	1.16	3.8	0.96	3.7	5.15	9.3
Defined benefit	1.14	3.1	1.33	3.7	0.95	2.6	0.51	1.7	0.46	1.8	3.76	6.8
Defined contribution	0.88	2.4	0.74	2.0	0.89	2.4	0.65	2.2	0.50	1.9	1.40	2.5
Legally required benefits	3.19	8.6	3.80	10.5	2.87	7.8	2.35	7.8	2.23	8.7	3.53	6.4
Social Security and Medicare	2.09	5.6	2.07	5.7	2.07	5.6	1.74	5.8	1.49	5.8	2.97	5.4
Social Security[6]	1.68	4.5	1.67	4.6	1.66	4.5	1.39	4.6	1.20	4.7	2.37	4.3
Medicare	0.41	1.1	0.40	1.1	0.41	1.1	0.35	1.2	0.29	1.1	0.60	1.1
Federal unemployment insurance	0.04	0.1	0.04	0.1	0.04	0.1	0.04	0.1	0.04	0.2	0.04	0.1
State unemployment insurance	0.28	0.7	0.38	1.0	0.24	0.7	0.20	0.7	0.18	0.7	0.24	0.4
Workers' compensation	0.78	2.1	1.32	3.6	0.53	1.5	0.37	1.2	0.51	2.0	0.29	0.5

See footnotes at end of table.

Table 6. Employer costs per hour worked for employee compensation and costs as a percent of total compensation: Private industry workers, by major industry group, December 2014 — Continued

Compensation component	Service-providing[2]									
	Financial activities		Professional and business services		Education and health services		Leisure and hospitality		Other services	
	Cost	Percent	Cost	Percent	Cost	Percent	Cost	Percent	Cost	Percent
Total compensation	$44.03	100.0	$38.49	100.0	$32.70	100.0	$13.19	100.0	$25.59	100.0
Wages and salaries	28.97	65.8	27.21	70.7	23.14	70.8	10.33	78.3	18.55	72.5
Total benefits	15.06	34.2	11.28	29.3	9.56	29.2	2.86	21.7	7.04	27.5
Paid leave	3.69	8.4	2.80	7.3	2.51	7.7	0.41	3.1	1.53	6.0
Vacation	1.92	4.4	1.47	3.8	1.26	3.9	0.22	1.7	0.73	2.9
Holiday	1.06	2.4	0.85	2.2	0.73	2.2	0.12	0.9	0.51	2.0
Sick	0.50	1.1	0.32	0.8	0.37	1.1	0.05	0.4	0.19	0.7
Personal	0.21	0.5	0.16	0.4	0.14	0.4	0.02	0.2	0.10	0.4
Supplemental pay	3.12	7.1	1.82	4.7	0.59	1.8	0.15	1.1	0.35	1.4
Overtime and premium[3]	0.17	0.4	0.22	0.6	0.18	0.6	0.07	0.5	0.14	0.6
Shift differentials	([4])	([5])	0.02	0.1	0.18	0.6	([4])	([5])	0.02	0.1
Nonproduction bonuses	2.94	6.7	1.58	4.1	0.22	0.7	0.07	0.5	0.19	0.7
Insurance	3.68	8.4	2.44	6.3	2.82	8.6	0.71	5.4	1.88	7.4
Life	0.05	0.1	0.05	0.1	0.04	0.1	([4])	([5])	0.03	0.1
Health	3.44	7.8	2.26	5.9	2.68	8.2	0.68	5.2	1.80	7.0
Short-term disability	0.12	0.3	0.06	0.2	0.04	0.1	([4])	([5])	0.03	0.1
Long-term disability	0.06	0.1	0.06	0.2	0.05	0.2	([4])	([5])	0.02	0.1
Retirement and savings	1.73	3.9	1.38	3.6	1.19	3.6	0.19	1.5	1.09	4.3
Defined benefit	0.49	1.1	0.57	1.5	0.40	1.2	0.08	0.6	0.60	2.4
Defined contribution	1.24	2.8	0.81	2.1	0.79	2.4	0.11	0.8	0.49	1.9
Legally required benefits	2.84	6.4	2.85	7.4	2.45	7.5	1.40	10.6	2.18	8.5
Social Security and Medicare	2.38	5.4	2.19	5.7	1.91	5.8	0.90	6.8	1.53	6.0
Social Security[6]	1.87	4.2	1.73	4.5	1.53	4.7	0.73	5.5	1.24	4.8
Medicare	0.51	1.2	0.46	1.2	0.38	1.2	0.17	1.3	0.30	1.2
Federal unemployment insurance	0.04	0.1	0.04	0.1	0.03	0.1	0.05	0.4	0.04	0.1
State unemployment insurance	0.22	0.5	0.25	0.6	0.19	0.6	0.18	1.4	0.22	0.9
Workers' compensation	0.20	0.5	0.37	1.0	0.32	1.0	0.27	2.1	0.39	1.5

[1] Includes mining, construction, and manufacturing. The agriculture, forestry, farming, and hunting sector is excluded.

[2] Includes utilities; wholesale trade; retail trade; transportation and warehousing; information; finance and insurance; real estate and rental and leasing; professional and technical services; management of companies and enterprises; administrative and waste services; educational services;   health care and social assistance; arts, entertainment and recreation; accommodation and food services; and other services, except public administration.

[3] Includes premium pay for work in addition to the regular work schedule (such as overtime, weekends, and holidays).

[4] Cost per hour worked is $0.01 or less.

[5] Less than .05 percent.

[6] Comprises the Old-Age, Survivors, and Disability Insurance (OASDI) program.

Note: The sum of individual items may not equal totals due to rounding.

- 13 -

Table 7. Employer costs per hour worked for employee compensation and costs as a percent of total compensation: Private industry workers, by census region and division, December 2014

Compensation component	Census region and division[1]									
	Northeast		Northeast divisions				South		South divisions	
			New England		Middle Atlantic				South Atlantic	
	Cost	Percent	Cost	Percent	Cost	Percent	Cost	Percent	Cost	Percent
Total compensation	$38.14	100.0	$37.12	100.0	$38.51	100.0	$28.81	100.0	$29.71	100.0
Wages and salaries	25.42	66.6	25.99	70.0	25.22	65.5	20.42	70.9	21.05	70.9
Total benefits	12.72	33.4	11.12	30.0	13.30	34.5	8.40	29.1	8.66	29.1
Paid leave	2.83	7.4	2.71	7.3	2.88	7.5	1.95	6.8	2.11	7.1
Vacation	1.44	3.8	1.42	3.8	1.45	3.8	1.02	3.5	1.10	3.7
Holiday	0.83	2.2	0.81	2.2	0.84	2.2	0.59	2.1	0.63	2.1
Sick	0.38	1.0	0.32	0.9	0.40	1.0	0.23	0.8	0.25	0.9
Personal	0.18	0.5	0.16	0.4	0.19	0.5	0.11	0.4	0.13	0.4
Supplemental pay	2.13	5.6	1.05	2.8	2.51	6.5	0.88	3.0	0.80	2.7
Overtime and premium[2]	0.25	0.7	0.27	0.7	0.25	0.6	0.29	1.0	0.23	0.8
Shift differentials	0.08	0.2	0.09	0.2	0.07	0.2	0.05	0.2	0.06	0.2
Nonproduction bonuses	1.80	4.7	0.69	1.9	2.19	5.7	0.53	1.9	0.51	1.7
Insurance	3.15	8.3	2.96	8.0	3.22	8.4	2.18	7.6	2.26	7.6
Life	0.05	0.1	0.04	0.1	0.05	0.1	0.05	0.2	0.05	0.2
Health	2.95	7.7	2.77	7.5	3.02	7.8	2.03	7.1	2.11	7.1
Short-term disability	0.09	0.2	0.09	0.2	0.10	0.3	0.05	0.2	0.06	0.2
Long-term disability	0.06	0.2	0.06	0.1	0.06	0.2	0.04	0.2	0.05	0.2
Retirement and savings	1.67	4.4	1.51	4.1	1.72	4.5	1.17	4.0	1.20	4.1
Defined benefit	0.77	2.0	0.68	1.8	0.81	2.1	0.55	1.9	0.55	1.9
Defined contribution	0.89	2.3	0.83	2.2	0.92	2.4	0.62	2.1	0.65	2.2
Legally required benefits	2.94	7.7	2.89	7.8	2.96	7.7	2.23	7.7	2.28	7.7
Social Security and Medicare	2.07	5.4	2.14	5.8	2.05	5.3	1.70	5.9	1.76	5.9
Social Security[3]	1.63	4.3	1.71	4.6	1.60	4.2	1.37	4.8	1.41	4.8
Medicare	0.44	1.2	0.43	1.2	0.44	1.2	0.34	1.2	0.35	1.2
Federal unemployment insurance	0.04	0.1	0.03	0.1	0.04	0.1	0.03	0.1	0.04	0.1
State unemployment insurance	0.32	0.8	0.31	0.8	0.32	0.8	0.15	0.5	0.15	0.5
Workers' compensation	0.51	1.3	0.40	1.1	0.55	1.4	0.35	1.2	0.34	1.1

See footnotes at end of table.

Table 7. Employer costs per hour worked for employee compensation and costs as a percent of total compensation: Private industry workers, by census region and division, December 2014 — Continued

Compensation component	Census region and division[1]									
	South divisions				Midwest		Midwest divisions			
	East South Central		West South Central		Cost	Percent	East North Central		West North Central	
	Cost	Percent	Cost	Percent			Cost	Percent	Cost	Percent
Total compensation	$24.88	100.0	$29.23	100.0	$28.85	100.0	$29.15	100.0	$28.26	100.0
Wages and salaries	17.68	71.0	20.68	70.8	20.00	69.3	20.08	68.9	19.86	70.3
Total benefits	7.21	29.0	8.54	29.2	8.85	30.7	9.07	31.1	8.41	29.7
Paid leave	1.59	6.4	1.85	6.3	1.97	6.8	1.97	6.7	1.98	7.0
Vacation	0.82	3.3	0.96	3.3	1.07	3.7	1.07	3.7	1.07	3.8
Holiday	0.52	2.1	0.57	2.0	0.60	2.1	0.60	2.0	0.60	2.1
Sick	0.18	0.7	0.21	0.7	0.21	0.7	0.20	0.7	0.22	0.8
Personal	0.07	0.3	0.11	0.4	0.10	0.3	0.10	0.3	0.09	0.3
Supplemental pay	0.70	2.8	1.10	3.8	0.79	2.7	0.86	3.0	0.65	2.3
Overtime and premium[2]	0.31	1.2	0.38	1.3	0.25	0.9	0.28	1.0	0.20	0.7
Shift differentials	0.04	0.1	0.05	0.2	0.06	0.2	0.07	0.2	0.06	0.2
Nonproduction bonuses	0.36	1.4	0.67	2.3	0.47	1.6	0.51	1.8	0.39	1.4
Insurance	2.09	8.4	2.06	7.1	2.58	8.9	2.63	9.0	2.46	8.7
Life	0.04	0.2	0.05	0.2	0.04	0.1	0.04	0.1	0.04	0.1
Health	1.97	7.9	1.93	6.6	2.43	8.4	2.49	8.5	2.32	8.2
Short-term disability	0.04	0.2	0.04	0.1	0.06	0.2	0.06	0.2	0.05	0.2
Long-term disability	0.05	0.2	0.04	0.1	0.05	0.2	0.05	0.2	0.05	0.2
Retirement and savings	0.82	3.3	1.27	4.3	1.17	4.1	1.22	4.2	1.08	3.8
Defined benefit	0.35	1.4	0.64	2.2	0.53	1.8	0.61	2.1	0.37	1.3
Defined contribution	0.47	1.9	0.63	2.2	0.64	2.2	0.61	2.1	0.71	2.5
Legally required benefits	2.00	8.0	2.26	7.7	2.34	8.1	2.39	8.2	2.24	7.9
Social Security and Medicare	1.50	6.0	1.72	5.9	1.69	5.9	1.70	5.8	1.67	5.9
Social Security[3]	1.21	4.9	1.38	4.7	1.36	4.7	1.37	4.7	1.34	4.8
Medicare	0.29	1.2	0.34	1.2	0.33	1.1	0.33	1.1	0.33	1.2
Federal unemployment insurance	0.03	0.1	0.03	0.1	0.04	0.2	0.05	0.2	0.04	0.1
State unemployment insurance	0.12	0.5	0.15	0.5	0.22	0.8	0.24	0.8	0.19	0.7
Workers' compensation	0.35	1.4	0.37	1.3	0.39	1.3	0.41	1.4	0.35	1.2

See footnotes at end of table.

Table 7. Employer costs per hour worked for employee compensation and costs as a percent of total compensation: Private industry workers, by census region and division, December 2014 — Continued

Compensation component	Census region and division[1]					
	West		West divisions			
			Mountain		Pacific	
	Cost	Percent	Cost	Percent	Cost	Percent
Total compensation	$32.08	100.0	$27.66	100.0	$34.14	100.0
Wages and salaries	22.48	70.1	19.88	71.9	23.69	69.4
Total benefits	9.60	29.9	7.78	28.1	10.45	30.6
Paid leave	2.12	6.6	1.71	6.2	2.32	6.8
Vacation	1.09	3.4	0.88	3.2	1.18	3.5
Holiday	0.66	2.1	0.53	1.9	0.73	2.1
Sick	0.28	0.9	0.21	0.7	0.31	0.9
Personal	0.09	0.3	0.10	0.3	0.09	0.3
Supplemental pay	0.90	2.8	0.73	2.6	0.97	2.9
Overtime and premium[2]	0.23	0.7	0.22	0.8	0.24	0.7
Shift differentials	0.05	0.2	0.03	0.1	0.06	0.2
Nonproduction bonuses	0.61	1.9	0.47	1.7	0.68	2.0
Insurance	2.53	7.9	2.15	7.8	2.70	7.9
Life	0.04	0.1	0.04	0.1	0.04	0.1
Health	2.41	7.5	2.04	7.4	2.59	7.6
Short-term disability	0.03	0.1	0.03	0.1	0.03	0.1
Long-term disability	0.04	0.1	0.04	0.2	0.04	0.1
Retirement and savings	1.36	4.2	0.95	3.4	1.55	4.5
Defined benefit	0.69	2.1	0.35	1.3	0.85	2.5
Defined contribution	0.67	2.1	0.60	2.2	0.70	2.1
Legally required benefits	2.70	8.4	2.24	8.1	2.91	8.5
Social Security and Medicare	1.85	5.8	1.65	6.0	1.94	5.7
Social Security[3]	1.48	4.6	1.33	4.8	1.55	4.5
Medicare	0.37	1.2	0.32	1.2	0.39	1.1
Federal unemployment insurance	0.05	0.1	0.03	0.1	0.05	0.2
State unemployment insurance	0.23	0.7	0.18	0.7	0.26	0.8
Workers' compensation	0.57	1.8	0.38	1.4	0.66	1.9

[1] The States that comprise the census divisions are: New England: Connecticut, Maine, Massachusetts, New Hampshire, Rhode Island and Vermont; Middle Atlantic: New Jersey, New York, and Pennsylvania; South Atlantic: Delaware, District of Columbia, Florida, Georgia, Maryland, North Carolina, South Carolina, Virginia, and West Virginia; East South Central: Alabama, Kentucky, Mississippi, and Tennessee; West South Central: Arkansas, Louisiana, Oklahoma, and Texas; East North Central: Illinois, Indiana, Michigan, Ohio, and Wisconsin; West North Central: Iowa, Kansas, Minnesota, Missouri, Nebraska, North Dakota, and South Dakota; Mountain: Arizona, Colorado, Idaho, Montana, Nevada, New Mexico, Utah, and Wyoming; and Pacific: Alaska, California, Hawaii, Oregon, and Washington.

[2] Includes premium pay for work in addition to the regular work schedule (such as overtime, weekends, and holidays).

[3] Comprises the Old-Age, Survivors, and Disability Insurance (OASDI) program.

Note: The sum of individual items may not equal totals due to rounding.

Table 8. Employer costs per hour worked for employee compensation and costs as a percent of total compensation: Private industry workers, by establishment employment size, December 2014

Compensation component	1-99 workers						100 workers or more					
	1-99 workers		1-49 workers		50-99 workers		100 workers or more		100-499 workers		500 workers or more	
	Cost	Percent	Cost	Percent	Cost	Percent	Cost	Percent	Cost	Percent	Cost	Percent
Total compensation	$26.23	100.0	$25.27	100.0	$29.22	100.0	$37.35	100.0	$31.64	100.0	$45.88	100.0
Wages and salaries	19.01	72.5	18.50	73.2	20.61	70.5	24.94	66.8	21.72	68.7	29.74	64.8
Total benefits	7.22	27.5	6.77	26.8	8.61	29.5	12.41	33.2	9.92	31.3	16.14	35.2
Paid leave	1.53	5.8	1.43	5.6	1.85	6.3	2.91	7.8	2.26	7.2	3.87	8.4
Vacation	0.78	3.0	0.73	2.9	0.94	3.2	1.53	4.1	1.20	3.8	2.04	4.4
Holiday	0.49	1.9	0.46	1.8	0.59	2.0	0.85	2.3	0.67	2.1	1.11	2.4
Sick	0.18	0.7	0.16	0.6	0.22	0.8	0.36	1.0	0.26	0.8	0.52	1.1
Personal	0.08	0.3	0.07	0.3	0.10	0.3	0.17	0.4	0.14	0.4	0.20	0.4
Supplemental pay	0.90	3.4	0.86	3.4	1.03	3.5	1.33	3.6	0.94	3.0	1.91	4.2
Overtime and premium[1]	0.18	0.7	0.17	0.7	0.23	0.8	0.35	0.9	0.33	1.0	0.39	0.8
Shift differentials	([2])	([3])	([2])	([3])	0.02	0.1	0.11	0.3	0.06	0.2	0.20	0.4
Nonproduction bonuses	0.71	2.7	0.69	2.7	0.78	2.7	0.86	2.3	0.55	1.8	1.32	2.9
Insurance	1.78	6.8	1.65	6.5	2.19	7.5	3.43	9.2	2.82	8.9	4.36	9.5
Life	0.03	0.1	0.03	0.1	0.04	0.1	0.06	0.2	0.05	0.2	0.07	0.2
Health	1.69	6.4	1.57	6.2	2.07	7.1	3.22	8.6	2.65	8.4	4.06	8.9
Short-term disability	0.03	0.1	0.03	0.1	0.04	0.1	0.09	0.2	0.07	0.2	0.11	0.2
Long-term disability	0.03	0.1	0.02	0.1	0.04	0.1	0.07	0.2	0.05	0.2	0.11	0.2
Retirement and savings	0.76	2.9	0.63	2.5	1.17	4.0	1.95	5.2	1.37	4.3	2.81	6.1
Defined benefit	0.32	1.2	0.25	1.0	0.54	1.9	0.97	2.6	0.65	2.0	1.45	3.2
Defined contribution	0.44	1.7	0.38	1.5	0.62	2.1	0.98	2.6	0.73	2.3	1.36	3.0
Legally required benefits	2.25	8.6	2.21	8.7	2.37	8.1	2.79	7.5	2.52	8.0	3.19	7.0
Social Security and Medicare	1.55	5.9	1.51	6.0	1.66	5.7	2.10	5.6	1.82	5.8	2.52	5.5
Social Security[4]	1.24	4.7	1.21	4.8	1.32	4.5	1.68	4.5	1.46	4.6	2.01	4.4
Medicare	0.31	1.2	0.30	1.2	0.34	1.2	0.42	1.1	0.36	1.1	0.51	1.1
Federal unemployment insurance ...	0.04	0.2	0.04	0.2	0.04	0.1	0.04	0.1	0.04	0.1	0.03	0.1
State unemployment insurance ...	0.22	0.8	0.21	0.8	0.23	0.8	0.22	0.6	0.22	0.7	0.21	0.5
Workers' compensation	0.44	1.7	0.44	1.7	0.44	1.5	0.44	1.2	0.44	1.4	0.43	0.9

[1] Includes premium pay for work in addition to the regular work schedule (such as overtime, weekends, and holidays).
[2] Cost per hour worked is $0.01 or less.
[3] Less than .05 percent.

[4] Comprises the Old-Age, Survivors, and Disability Insurance (OASDI) program.

Note: The sum of individual items may not equal totals due to rounding.

Table 9. Employer costs per hour worked for employee compensation and costs as a percent of total compensation: Private industry workers, goods-producing and service-providing industries, by occupational group, December 2014

Series	Total compen-sation	Wages and salaries	Benefit costs					
			Total	Paid leave	Supple-mental pay	Insurance	Retire-ment and savings	Legally required benefits
	Cost per hour worked							
All workers in private industry	$31.32	$21.72	$9.60	$2.16	$1.10	$2.54	$1.30	$2.50
Management, professional, and related	55.56	38.14	17.42	4.67	2.45	3.94	2.70	3.66
Management, business, and financial	66.57	44.52	22.04	5.89	4.46	4.33	3.27	4.09
Professional and related	49.50	34.63	14.87	4.00	1.35	3.72	2.38	3.43
Sales and office	23.57	16.81	6.76	1.48	0.58	2.14	0.70	1.86
Sales and related	22.96	17.23	5.72	1.27	0.57	1.51	0.53	1.84
Office and administrative support	23.98	16.52	7.46	1.62	0.59	2.57	0.81	1.88
Service	14.38	10.93	3.45	0.56	0.24	0.90	0.24	1.52
Natural resources, construction, and maintenance	34.15	22.76	11.39	1.79	1.03	3.08	2.16	3.33
Construction, extraction, farming, fishing, and forestry[1]	34.82	23.10	11.72	1.33	0.95	3.11	2.51	3.82
Installation, maintenance, and repair	33.60	22.48	11.12	2.17	1.09	3.05	1.87	2.93
Production, transportation, and material moving	26.83	17.67	9.16	1.63	1.01	2.86	1.09	2.57
Production	26.32	17.44	8.88	1.65	1.15	2.80	0.89	2.39
Transportation and material moving	27.31	17.89	9.42	1.61	0.87	2.92	1.28	2.75
All workers, goods-producing industries[2]	37.21	24.61	12.60	2.44	1.49	3.46	2.02	3.19
Management, professional, and related	66.55	44.31	22.24	5.70	2.79	4.80	4.60	4.35
Sales and office	30.09	20.91	9.18	2.05	0.80	2.99	0.94	2.40
Natural resources, construction, and maintenance	35.59	23.45	12.14	1.52	1.17	3.26	2.40	3.79
Production, transportation, and material moving	27.59	17.90	9.69	1.71	1.30	3.17	0.97	2.54
All workers, service-providing industries[3]	30.10	21.13	8.98	2.10	1.02	2.34	1.16	2.35
Management, professional, and related	54.00	37.27	16.74	4.53	2.40	3.81	2.43	3.57
Sales and office	23.08	16.50	6.58	1.43	0.56	2.07	0.68	1.82
Service	14.33	10.90	3.43	0.55	0.23	0.90	0.23	1.51
Natural resources, construction, and maintenance	32.49	21.97	10.52	2.11	0.86	2.86	1.88	2.80
Production, transportation, and material moving	26.21	17.49	8.72	1.57	0.77	2.61	1.18	2.60
	Percent of total compensation							
All workers in private industry	100.0	69.4	30.6	6.9	3.5	8.1	4.2	8.0
Management, professional, and related	100.0	68.6	31.4	8.4	4.4	7.1	4.9	6.6
Management, business, and financial	100.0	66.9	33.1	8.8	6.7	6.5	4.9	6.2
Professional and related	100.0	70.0	30.0	8.1	2.7	7.5	4.8	6.9
Sales and office	100.0	71.3	28.7	6.3	2.5	9.1	3.0	7.9
Sales and related	100.0	75.1	24.9	5.5	2.5	6.6	2.3	8.0
Office and administrative support	100.0	68.9	31.1	6.7	2.4	10.7	3.4	7.8
Service	100.0	76.0	24.0	3.9	1.6	6.3	1.6	10.6
Natural resources, construction, and maintenance	100.0	66.7	33.3	5.2	3.0	9.0	6.3	9.8
Construction, extraction, farming, fishing, and forestry[1]	100.0	66.4	33.6	3.8	2.7	8.9	7.2	11.0
Installation, maintenance, and repair	100.0	66.9	33.1	6.5	3.2	9.1	5.6	8.7
Production, transportation, and material moving	100.0	65.9	34.1	6.1	3.8	10.7	4.0	9.6
Production	100.0	66.3	33.7	6.3	4.4	10.6	3.4	9.1
Transportation and material moving	100.0	65.5	34.5	5.9	3.2	10.7	4.7	10.1
All workers, goods-producing industries[2]	100.0	66.1	33.9	6.6	4.0	9.3	5.4	8.6
Management, professional, and related	100.0	66.6	33.4	8.6	4.2	7.2	6.9	6.5
Sales and office	100.0	69.5	30.5	6.8	2.6	10.0	3.1	8.0
Natural resources, construction, and maintenance	100.0	65.9	34.1	4.3	3.3	9.2	6.7	10.7
Production, transportation, and material moving	100.0	64.9	35.1	6.2	4.7	11.5	3.5	9.2
All workers, service-providing industries[3]	100.0	70.2	29.8	7.0	3.4	7.8	3.8	7.8
Management, professional, and related	100.0	69.0	31.0	8.4	4.4	7.1	4.5	6.6
Sales and office	100.0	71.5	28.5	6.2	2.4	9.0	3.0	7.9
Service	100.0	76.1	23.9	3.9	1.6	6.3	1.6	10.6
Natural resources, construction, and maintenance	100.0	67.6	32.4	6.5	2.6	8.8	5.8	8.6
Production, transportation, and material moving	100.0	66.7	33.3	6.0	2.9	10.0	4.5	9.9

[1] Farming, fishing, and forestry occupations were combined with construction and extraction occupational group as of December 2006.
[2] Includes mining, construction, and manufacturing. The agriculture, forestry, farming, and hunting sector is excluded.
[3] Includes utilities; wholesale trade; retail trade; transportation and warehousing; information; finance and insurance; real estate and rental and leasing; professional and technical services; management of companies and enterprises; administrative and waste services; educational services; health care and social assistance; arts, entertainment and recreation; accommodation and food services; and other services, except public administration.

Note: The sum of individual items may not equal totals due to rounding.

Table 10. Employer costs per hour worked for employee compensation and costs as a percent of total compensation: Private industry workers, by industry group, December 2014

Series	Total compen-sation	Wages and salaries	Benefit costs					
			Total	Paid leave	Supple-mental pay	Insurance	Retire-ment and savings	Legally required benefits
	Cost per hour worked							
All workers, goods-producing industries[1]	$37.21	$24.61	$12.60	$2.44	$1.49	$3.46	$2.02	$3.19
Construction	36.31	24.97	11.34	1.59	0.96	2.92	2.07	3.80
Manufacturing	36.73	23.95	12.78	2.77	1.62	3.68	1.84	2.87
Aircraft manufacturing[2]	68.97	40.73	28.24	5.99	4.89	6.88	6.23	4.26
All workers, service-providing industries[3]	30.10	21.13	8.98	2.10	1.02	2.34	1.16	2.35
Trade, transportation, and utilities	25.74	18.10	7.64	1.60	0.64	2.22	0.96	2.23
Wholesale trade	34.34	24.19	10.15	2.45	1.02	2.91	1.04	2.72
Retail trade	17.91	13.52	4.39	0.83	0.29	1.26	0.39	1.62
Transportation and warehousing	38.04	24.28	13.75	2.76	1.18	4.18	2.17	3.46
Utilities	61.42	37.68	23.74	5.49	2.09	6.05	5.94	4.17
Information	55.44	34.31	21.13	4.82	2.42	5.20	5.15	3.53
Financial activities	44.03	28.97	15.06	3.69	3.12	3.68	1.73	2.84
Finance and insurance	48.62	31.53	17.09	4.23	3.85	4.04	2.01	2.97
Credit intermediation and related activities	39.69	26.62	13.07	3.51	1.77	3.61	1.59	2.59
Insurance carriers and related activities	44.80	29.67	15.13	3.95	1.94	4.10	2.20	2.94
Real estate and rental and leasing	28.92	20.54	8.38	1.94	0.73	2.50	0.81	2.40
Professional and business services	38.49	27.21	11.28	2.80	1.82	2.44	1.38	2.85
Professional and technical services	48.47	34.62	13.86	4.10	1.31	3.27	1.84	3.34
Administrative and waste services	22.48	17.12	5.36	1.01	0.50	1.21	0.47	2.16
Education and health services	32.70	23.14	9.56	2.51	0.59	2.82	1.19	2.45
Educational services	41.84	30.36	11.48	2.93	0.23	3.42	1.92	2.97
Junior colleges, colleges, and universities	50.76	35.94	14.82	4.07	0.27	4.35	2.73	3.39
Health care and social assistance	31.22	21.97	9.25	2.44	0.65	2.72	1.07	2.37
Leisure and hospitality	13.19	10.33	2.86	0.41	0.15	0.71	0.19	1.40
Accommodation and food services	11.99	9.49	2.50	0.31	0.13	0.60	0.14	1.32
Other services	25.59	18.55	7.04	1.53	0.35	1.88	1.09	2.18
	Percent of total compensation							
All workers, goods-producing industries[1]	100.0	66.1	33.9	6.6	4.0	9.3	5.4	8.6
Construction	100.0	68.8	31.2	4.4	2.6	8.1	5.7	10.5
Manufacturing	100.0	65.2	34.8	7.6	4.4	10.0	5.0	7.8
Aircraft manufacturing[2]	100.0	59.1	40.9	8.7	7.1	10.0	9.0	6.2
All workers, service-providing industries[3]	100.0	70.2	29.8	7.0	3.4	7.8	3.8	7.8
Trade, transportation, and utilities	100.0	70.3	29.7	6.2	2.5	8.6	3.7	8.7
Wholesale trade	100.0	70.5	29.5	7.1	3.0	8.5	3.0	7.9
Retail trade	100.0	75.5	24.5	4.6	1.6	7.1	2.2	9.0
Transportation and warehousing	100.0	63.8	36.2	7.3	3.1	11.0	5.7	9.1
Utilities	100.0	61.3	38.7	8.9	3.4	9.8	9.7	6.8
Information	100.0	61.9	38.1	8.7	4.4	9.4	9.3	6.4
Financial activities	100.0	65.8	34.2	8.4	7.1	8.4	3.9	6.4
Finance and insurance	100.0	64.8	35.2	8.7	7.0	8.3	4.1	6.1
Credit intermediation and related activities	100.0	67.1	32.9	8.8	4.5	9.1	4.0	6.5
Insurance carriers and related activities	100.0	66.2	33.8	8.8	4.3	9.2	4.9	6.6
Real estate and rental and leasing	100.0	71.0	29.0	6.7	2.5	8.7	2.8	8.3
Professional and business services	100.0	70.7	29.3	7.3	4.7	6.3	3.6	7.4
Professional and technical services	100.0	71.4	28.6	8.5	2.7	6.8	3.8	6.9
Administrative and waste services	100.0	76.2	23.8	4.5	2.2	5.4	2.1	9.6
Education and health services	100.0	70.8	29.2	7.7	1.8	8.6	3.6	7.5
Educational services	100.0	72.6	27.4	7.0	0.6	8.2	4.6	7.1
Junior colleges, colleges, and universities	100.0	70.8	29.2	8.0	0.5	8.6	5.4	6.7
Health care and social assistance	100.0	70.4	29.6	7.8	2.1	8.7	3.4	7.6
Leisure and hospitality	100.0	78.3	21.7	3.1	1.1	5.4	1.5	10.6
Accommodation and food services	100.0	79.1	20.9	2.6	1.1	5.0	1.2	11.0
Other services	100.0	72.5	27.5	6.0	1.4	7.4	4.3	8.5

[1] Includes mining, construction, and manufacturing. The agriculture, forestry, farming, and hunting sector is excluded.
[2] Data are available beginning with December 2006.
[3] Includes utilities; wholesale trade; retail trade; transportation and warehousing; information; finance and insurance; real estate and rental and leasing; professional and technical services; management of companies and enterprises; administrative and waste services; educational services; health care and social assistance; arts, entertainment and recreation; accommodation and food services; and other services, except public administration.

Note: The sum of individual items may not equal totals due to rounding.

Table 11. Employer costs per hour worked for employee compensation and costs as a percent of total compensation: Private industry workers, by occupational group and full-time and part-time status, December 2014

Series	Total compen-sation	Wages and salaries	Benefit costs					
			Total	Paid leave	Supple-mental pay	Insurance	Retire-ment and savings	Legally required benefits
			Cost per hour worked					
All full-time workers in private industry	$36.70	$24.91	$11.80	$2.77	$1.41	$3.18	$1.65	$2.78
Management, professional, and related	58.00	39.31	18.69	5.08	2.67	4.26	2.94	3.73
Management, business, and financial	67.34	44.90	22.44	5.99	4.57	4.41	3.35	4.12
Professional and related	51.96	35.69	16.27	4.49	1.45	4.17	2.68	3.49
Sales and office	27.90	19.38	8.52	1.99	0.78	2.78	0.91	2.07
Sales and related	31.89	23.28	8.60	2.15	0.96	2.33	0.84	2.32
Office and administrative support	26.04	17.56	8.48	1.91	0.70	2.98	0.93	1.96
Service	17.71	12.64	5.07	0.99	0.39	1.59	0.39	1.70
Natural resources, construction, and maintenance	34.83	23.10	11.74	1.87	1.06	3.20	2.23	3.37
Construction, extraction, farming, fishing, and forestry[1]	35.57	23.49	12.07	1.39	0.99	3.23	2.59	3.87
Installation, maintenance, and repair	34.23	22.77	11.46	2.26	1.12	3.17	1.94	2.96
Production, transportation, and material moving	28.77	18.82	9.94	1.84	1.14	3.13	1.16	2.66
Production	27.12	17.83	9.29	1.74	1.22	2.96	0.94	2.43
Transportation and material moving	30.75	20.02	10.73	1.97	1.05	3.33	1.43	2.94
All part-time workers in private industry	16.09	12.72	3.37	0.45	0.22	0.70	0.32	1.68
Management, professional, and related	37.92	29.70	8.22	1.73	0.85	1.56	0.93	3.14
Professional and related	37.66	29.51	8.15	1.68	0.85	1.54	0.94	3.14
Sales and office	13.69	10.94	2.75	0.32	0.12	0.69	0.24	1.39
Sales and related	12.17	9.93	2.24	0.22	0.09	0.51	0.16	1.26
Office and administrative support	15.97	12.45	3.52	0.48	0.16	0.95	0.35	1.59
Service	11.40	9.39	2.01	0.18	0.09	0.29	0.10	1.35
Production, transportation, and material moving	17.00	11.83	5.17	0.54	0.31	1.50	0.70	2.11
Transportation and material moving	17.50	11.82	5.69	0.58	0.34	1.75	0.83	2.18
			Percent of total compensation					
All full-time workers in private industry	100.0	67.9	32.1	7.5	3.8	8.7	4.5	7.6
Management, professional, and related	100.0	67.8	32.2	8.8	4.6	7.4	5.1	6.4
Management, business, and financial	100.0	66.7	33.3	8.9	6.8	6.5	5.0	6.1
Professional and related	100.0	68.7	31.3	8.6	2.8	8.0	5.2	6.7
Sales and office	100.0	69.5	30.5	7.1	2.8	9.9	3.2	7.4
Sales and related	100.0	73.0	27.0	6.7	3.0	7.3	2.6	7.3
Office and administrative support	100.0	67.4	32.6	7.3	2.7	11.5	3.6	7.5
Service	100.0	71.4	28.6	5.6	2.2	9.0	2.2	9.6
Natural resources, construction, and maintenance	100.0	66.3	33.7	5.4	3.1	9.2	6.4	9.7
Construction, extraction, farming, fishing, and forestry[1]	100.0	66.1	33.9	3.9	2.8	9.1	7.3	10.9
Installation, maintenance, and repair	100.0	66.5	33.5	6.6	3.3	9.3	5.7	8.7
Production, transportation, and material moving	100.0	65.4	34.6	6.4	4.0	10.9	4.0	9.3
Production	100.0	65.7	34.3	6.4	4.5	10.9	3.5	9.0
Transportation and material moving	100.0	65.1	34.9	6.4	3.4	10.8	4.7	9.6
All part-time workers in private industry	100.0	79.0	21.0	2.8	1.4	4.4	2.0	10.5
Management, professional, and related	100.0	78.3	21.7	4.6	2.2	4.1	2.5	8.3
Professional and related	100.0	78.3	21.7	4.5	2.3	4.1	2.5	8.3
Sales and office	100.0	79.9	20.1	2.3	0.9	5.0	1.7	10.2
Sales and related	100.0	81.6	18.4	1.8	0.7	4.2	1.3	10.4
Office and administrative support	100.0	78.0	22.0	3.0	1.0	5.9	2.2	9.9
Service	100.0	82.4	17.6	1.5	0.8	2.5	0.9	11.9
Production, transportation, and material moving	100.0	69.6	30.4	3.2	1.8	8.9	4.1	12.4
Transportation and material moving	100.0	67.5	32.5	3.3	2.0	10.0	4.8	12.5

[1] Farming, fishing, and forestry occupations were combined with construction and extraction occupational group as of December 2006.

Note: The sum of individual items may not equal totals due to rounding.

Table 12. Employer costs per hour worked for employee compensation and costs as a percent of total compensation: Private industry workers, by industry group and full-time and part-time status, December 2014

Series	Total compen-sation	Wages and salaries	Benefit costs					
			Total	Paid leave	Supple-mental pay	Insurance	Retire-ment and savings	Legally required benefits
	Cost per hour worked							
All full-time workers in private industry	$36.70	$24.91	$11.80	$2.77	$1.41	$3.18	$1.65	$2.78
Goods-producing[1]	37.77	24.90	12.86	2.51	1.52	3.56	2.07	3.21
Construction	36.98	25.33	11.65	1.66	0.99	3.05	2.13	3.82
Manufacturing	37.23	24.22	13.01	2.83	1.64	3.75	1.88	2.90
Service-providing[2]	36.40	24.91	11.49	2.84	1.38	3.08	1.53	2.66
Trade, transportation, and utilities	32.06	22.10	9.96	2.27	0.89	2.89	1.28	2.62
Information	57.96	35.67	22.28	5.09	2.56	5.49	5.48	3.66
Financial activities	46.39	30.34	16.04	3.97	3.38	3.89	1.86	2.94
Professional and business services	42.27	29.39	12.88	3.29	2.08	2.87	1.63	3.00
Education and health services	35.17	24.28	10.90	2.97	0.66	3.39	1.39	2.48
Leisure and hospitality	18.35	13.38	4.97	0.95	0.32	1.58	0.43	1.69
Other services	29.89	21.13	8.75	2.13	0.47	2.49	1.28	2.39
All part-time workers in private industry	16.09	12.72	3.37	0.45	0.22	0.70	0.32	1.68
Service-providing[2]	15.94	12.62	3.32	0.45	0.21	0.70	0.31	1.66
Trade, transportation, and utilities	14.07	10.72	3.36	0.36	0.16	0.97	0.36	1.50
Professional and business services	19.75	16.43	3.33	0.33	0.50	0.30	0.13	2.06
Education and health services	25.96	20.04	5.92	1.25	0.42	1.25	0.64	2.36
Leisure and hospitality	9.91	8.39	1.52	0.07	0.03	0.15	0.04	1.22
	Percent of total compensation							
All full-time workers in private industry	100.0	67.9	32.1	7.5	3.8	8.7	4.5	7.6
Goods-producing[1]	100.0	65.9	34.1	6.6	4.0	9.4	5.5	8.5
Construction	100.0	68.5	31.5	4.5	2.7	8.2	5.8	10.3
Manufacturing	100.0	65.1	34.9	7.6	4.4	10.1	5.0	7.8
Service-providing[2]	100.0	68.4	31.6	7.8	3.8	8.5	4.2	7.3
Trade, transportation, and utilities	100.0	68.9	31.1	7.1	2.8	9.0	4.0	8.2
Information	100.0	61.5	38.5	8.8	4.4	9.5	9.5	6.3
Financial activities	100.0	65.4	34.6	8.6	7.3	8.4	4.0	6.3
Professional and business services	100.0	69.5	30.5	7.8	4.9	6.8	3.9	7.1
Education and health services	100.0	69.0	31.0	8.5	1.9	9.6	3.9	7.1
Leisure and hospitality	100.0	72.9	27.1	5.2	1.8	8.6	2.3	9.2
Other services	100.0	70.7	29.3	7.1	1.6	8.3	4.3	8.0
All part-time workers in private industry	100.0	79.0	21.0	2.8	1.4	4.4	2.0	10.5
Service-providing[2]	100.0	79.2	20.8	2.8	1.3	4.4	1.9	10.4
Trade, transportation, and utilities	100.0	76.2	23.8	2.5	1.2	6.9	2.6	10.7
Professional and business services	100.0	83.2	16.8	1.7	2.5	1.5	0.7	10.4
Education and health services	100.0	77.2	22.8	4.8	1.6	4.8	2.4	9.1
Leisure and hospitality	100.0	84.7	15.3	0.7	0.3	1.5	0.4	12.4

[1] Includes mining, construction, and manufacturing. The agriculture, forestry, farming, and hunting sector is excluded.
[2] Includes utilities; wholesale trade; retail trade; transportation and warehousing; information; finance and insurance; real estate and rental and leasing; professional and technical services; management of companies and enterprises; administrative and waste services; educational services; health care and social assistance; arts, entertainment and recreation; accommodation and food services; and other services, except public administration.

Note: The sum of individual items may not equal totals due to rounding.

Table 13. Employer costs per hour worked for employee compensation and costs as a percent of total compensation: Private industry workers, by major industry group and establishment employment size and bargaining unit status, December 2014

Series	Total compensation	Wages and salaries	Benefit costs					
			Total	Paid leave	Supplemental pay	Insurance	Retirement and savings	Legally required benefits
Cost per hour worked								
All workers, goods-producing industries[1] ...	$37.21	$24.61	$12.60	$2.44	$1.49	$3.46	$2.02	$3.19
1-99 workers	31.12	21.87	9.25	1.60	0.91	2.52	1.16	3.07
1-49 workers	30.12	21.43	8.68	1.42	0.88	2.23	1.07	3.08
50-99 workers	33.69	22.99	10.70	2.05	0.98	3.25	1.40	3.03
100 workers or more	42.30	26.90	15.40	3.15	1.97	4.26	2.74	3.29
100-499 workers	36.57	23.91	12.66	2.49	1.42	3.83	1.76	3.16
500 workers or more	50.62	31.23	19.38	4.10	2.77	4.87	4.17	3.47
Union	46.10	26.85	19.25	2.54	1.69	6.19	4.76	4.08
Nonunion	35.38	24.15	11.23	2.42	1.44	2.91	1.46	3.00
All workers, service-providing industries[2] ..	30.10	21.13	8.98	2.10	1.02	2.34	1.16	2.35
1-99 workers	25.41	18.53	6.88	1.52	0.90	1.65	0.69	2.11
1-49 workers	24.50	18.03	6.47	1.43	0.86	1.55	0.56	2.07
50-99 workers	28.32	20.13	8.19	1.81	1.04	1.98	1.12	2.24
100 workers or more	36.09	24.44	11.65	2.85	1.17	3.22	1.75	2.66
100-499 workers	30.40	21.17	9.23	2.21	0.82	2.56	1.28	2.36
500 workers or more	44.64	29.35	15.29	3.81	1.68	4.22	2.45	3.12
Union	46.70	28.20	18.49	3.60	1.31	5.93	4.20	3.46
Nonunion	28.81	20.57	8.23	1.99	1.00	2.06	0.92	2.27
Percent of total compensation								
All workers, goods-producing industries[1] ...	100.0	66.1	33.9	6.6	4.0	9.3	5.4	8.6
1-99 workers	100.0	70.3	29.7	5.1	2.9	8.1	3.7	9.9
1-49 workers	100.0	71.2	28.8	4.7	2.9	7.4	3.5	10.2
50-99 workers	100.0	68.2	31.8	6.1	2.9	9.6	4.1	9.0
100 workers or more	100.0	63.6	36.4	7.4	4.7	10.1	6.5	7.8
100-499 workers	100.0	65.4	34.6	6.8	3.9	10.5	4.8	8.6
500 workers or more	100.0	61.7	38.3	8.1	5.5	9.6	8.2	6.9
Union	100.0	58.2	41.8	5.5	3.7	13.4	10.3	8.9
Nonunion	100.0	68.3	31.7	6.8	4.1	8.2	4.1	8.5
All workers, service-providing industries[2] ..	100.0	70.2	29.8	7.0	3.4	7.8	3.8	7.8
1-99 workers	100.0	72.9	27.1	6.0	3.6	6.5	2.7	8.3
1-49 workers	100.0	73.6	26.4	5.8	3.5	6.3	2.3	8.5
50-99 workers	100.0	71.1	28.9	6.4	3.7	7.0	4.0	7.9
100 workers or more	100.0	67.7	32.3	7.9	3.2	8.9	4.8	7.4
100-499 workers	100.0	69.6	30.4	7.3	2.7	8.4	4.2	7.8
500 workers or more	100.0	65.7	34.3	8.5	3.8	9.5	5.5	7.0
Union	100.0	60.4	39.6	7.7	2.8	12.7	9.0	7.4
Nonunion	100.0	71.4	28.6	6.9	3.5	7.2	3.2	7.9

[1] Includes mining, construction, and manufacturing. The agriculture, forestry, farming, and hunting sector is excluded.
[2] Includes utilities; wholesale trade; retail trade; transportation and warehousing; information; finance and insurance; real estate and rental and leasing; professional and technical services; management of companies and enterprises; administrative and waste services; educational services; health care and social assistance; arts, entertainment and recreation; accommodation and food services; and other services, except public administration.

Note: The sum of individual items may not equal totals due to rounding.

Table 14. Employer costs per hour worked for employee compensation and costs as a percent of total compensation: Private industry health care and social assistance workers, by industry and occupational group, December 2014

Series	Total compen-sation	Wages and salaries	Benefit costs					
			Total	Paid leave	Supple-mental pay	Insurance	Retire-ment and savings	Legally required benefits
Cost per hour worked								
Health care and social assistance	$31.22	$21.97	$9.25	$2.44	$0.65	$2.72	$1.07	$2.37
Management, professional, and related	44.33	31.06	13.27	3.77	0.93	3.65	1.82	3.11
Registered nurses	51.03	34.99	16.05	4.37	1.68	4.19	2.14	3.67
Sales and office	22.31	15.61	6.69	1.60	0.32	2.56	0.51	1.71
Service	17.91	12.85	5.06	1.05	0.44	1.56	0.34	1.66
Hospitals	41.99	27.83	14.16	3.75	1.44	4.21	1.78	2.97
Management, professional, and related	51.23	34.35	16.88	4.74	1.75	4.59	2.23	3.56
Registered nurses	54.06	35.94	18.12	4.91	2.19	4.76	2.46	3.80
Service	22.90	14.53	8.37	1.64	0.99	3.09	0.83	1.81
Nursing and residential care facilities	21.29	15.29	6.00	1.44	0.43	1.85	0.32	1.94
Management, professional, and related	32.62	23.64	8.97	2.43	0.59	2.65	0.62	2.69
Service	16.14	11.52	4.62	0.99	0.38	1.45	0.20	1.60
Nursing care facilities[1]	23.37	16.64	6.73	1.64	0.52	2.06	0.41	2.09
Management, professional, and related	36.17	26.15	10.02	2.72	0.71	2.85	0.77	2.96
Service	17.04	11.94	5.10	1.09	0.45	1.66	0.24	1.66
Percent of total compensation								
Health care and social assistance	100.0	70.4	29.6	7.8	2.1	8.7	3.4	7.6
Management, professional, and related	100.0	70.1	29.9	8.5	2.1	8.2	4.1	7.0
Registered nurses	100.0	68.6	31.4	8.6	3.3	8.2	4.2	7.2
Sales and office	100.0	70.0	30.0	7.2	1.4	11.5	2.3	7.7
Service	100.0	71.8	28.2	5.9	2.5	8.7	1.9	9.3
Hospitals	100.0	66.3	33.7	8.9	3.4	10.0	4.2	7.1
Management, professional, and related	100.0	67.1	32.9	9.3	3.4	9.0	4.4	6.9
Registered nurses	100.0	66.5	33.5	9.1	4.1	8.8	4.6	7.0
Service	100.0	63.5	36.5	7.1	4.3	13.5	3.6	7.9
Nursing and residential care facilities	100.0	71.8	28.2	6.8	2.0	8.7	1.5	9.1
Management, professional, and related	100.0	72.5	27.5	7.4	1.8	8.1	1.9	8.2
Service	100.0	71.4	28.6	6.1	2.4	9.0	1.2	9.9
Nursing care facilities[1]	100.0	71.2	28.8	7.0	2.2	8.8	1.8	8.9
Management, professional, and related	100.0	72.3	27.7	7.5	2.0	7.9	2.1	8.2
Service	100.0	70.1	29.9	6.4	2.7	9.7	1.4	9.7

[1] Data are available beginning with December 2006.

Note: The sum of individual items may not equal totals due to rounding.